Working Voices

by

Thomas Heffernan

ISBN-13: 978-1515313175
ISBN-10: 1515313174

UNIVERSITY
PRESS

St. Andrews University Press

St. Andrews University
(A branch of Webber International University)
1700 Dogwood Mile
Laurinburg, NC 28352
press@sa.edu
(910) 277-5310

Editorial Board

Paul Baldasare
Joseph Bathanti
Betsy Dendy
Robert Hopkins
Edna Ann Loftus
Madge McKeithen
Ted Wojtasik

Ted Wojtasik, Acting Editor

Ronald H. Bayes, Founding Editor
1969

Also by Thomas Heffernan

Mobiles (1974)

A Narrative of Jeremy Bentham (1978)

The Liam Poems (1981)

City Renewing Itself (1983)

Art and Emblem: 17ᵗʰ Century Emblems (1991)

Gathering in Ireland (1996)

White Edge, Curling Wave (2002)

Christmas Gifts in South Japan: Haiku Essays (2003)

<u>Editor</u>

A Poem is a Smile You Can Hear (1976)

International Poetry Review (1979)

Plover/Chidori (1990)

<u>Drama</u>

"Some Rise, Some Fall" (one-act play, 1959)

Available online:

http://nc-haiku.org/pdf/Heffernan_JapanTrip_2006.pdf

http://ncartseveryday.org/2011/09/nc-poets-on-911-tom-heffernan%E2%80%99s-%E2%80%9Csoon-it-will-be-ten-years%E2%80%9D/

For You, The Reader

Hence poetry is something more philosophic and of graver import than history, since its statements are of the nature rather of universals, whereas those of history are singulars. By a universal statement I mean [a statement] as to what such or such a kind of man will probably or necessarily say or do—which is the aim of poetry...

—Aristotle

Far and away the best prize life has to offer is the chance to work hard at work worth doing.

—Theodore Roosevelt

A Prefatory Note

More than twenty-five years ago something I read in Thomas Merton about language and solidarity led to reflection about social justice and about people without whom ordinary (and some extraordinary) daily life would not happen. Plumber, waitress, hairdresser, house painter, teacher, banker, temp worker are among those heard in these sonnet monologues whose manner—reminiscent of Aristotle's description, above—is likewise accountable in terms I observe in Anthony Trollope, "... real portraits, not of individuals known to the world or to the author, but of created personages impregnated with traits of character which are known."

Having heard some of these poems read aloud during annual Sensoria performances at Central Piedmont Community College in Charlotte, NC, my friend the art professor Elizabeth Ross has referred to them as "vignettes." (I adapt Wikipedia's definition: "short impressionistic scenes that focus on one moment or give a trenchant impression about a character, idea, setting, or object.")

And, here, a perspective is that human contexts are political; that even "created personages" may point to connectivity and our need of progressive policy.

So: progressive sonnet vignettes, *Working Voices*.

—T.H.

Table of Contents

TEMP, BEGINNING

Wait a minute, I've got a call, think what
I should put in my resumé. Temp work,
always low-wage—managing a budget,
that's a skill. No, I applied for bank clerk.

They said I was overqualified, two
degrees. Wait a minute, I've got a call.

The tall guy in the support group told me
he had good luck with house repair the fall
and winter, yard work spring and summer.
He wasn't fired, found out law wasn't him.
Kept the doctorate quiet, no employer
took him just the same. Tomorrow is gym.
Entrepreneurship tonight, evening school.
You want to go? Later. I've got a call.

WAITRESS, CLEARING

The people with two toddlers and the baby
in the highchair left mess per usual,
bones and chicken skin from the fricassee
on the two dinner plates, the kids crumble
their bun and hamburger bits, leave ketchup
blopped on the tabletop. The little one
upchucked on the highchair lid. A napkin
soaked up most of it, not much now to mop.

Her little pinafore was pretty pink
entirely, until she stuck her finger
in her mashed potato and dabbled it
on the front. She had a good time, I think.
Enjoyed it. All in a day's work. Some linger.
They left quick. One more table. Then I'll sit.

TEACHER

I don't really want to retire, but here
in this district, when you're seventy-five,
it's a rule. In June, my fiftieth year
in kindergarten, it's hard to believe.
My very first day half the children cried.
I wanted to go home like them to mother.
That first year we had a blizzard. I tried
hard, with boots, mittens. Nowadays, no bother.
They've already learned how from *Sesame Street*.
At first I thought *Mr. Rogers* silly.
It grew on me; the children enjoy it
and I'm truly glad. The years have changed me,
all this time with the young. I'm elementary,
my husband jokes, but it's the truth really.

CLEANER

Don't mind if we talk while I work, do you,
our schedule, you know, is tight. Help me push
back this desk? Thanks. It's not always a rush
like this, I'm the boss, a man has the flu.
This company's mine, so I fill in, jack
of all work, bookkeeper, paymaster, clerk.
Do a room this size in ten minutes, vac
takes five, dust and wastepaper baskets, jerk
out the plug, the rest. I have the crews wear
decent jackets and pants like I do. Used to,
when I taught school, a habit. A cleaner
should look clean, better image, I think so.
Bought a boat last winter, want to go cruise
a little. Relax. Heart. No cigarettes, booze.

ER Resident

You'll feel a quick little prick when I stick
the needle in, a little pain before
it goes numb. You don't feel it anymore?
There'll be a little pressure now. The trick
is keep your arm real still and let me know
so nothing hurts. I'm just going to start
slow and go from there. I've got the first part.
More local? Some will dribble. Here we go.

Well, that next bit took just a snip. We'll blot
and irrigate and then sew her up, only
will take three stitches. Good. You'll be on time
for your wedding, looks like, right on the dot
of three. You feel okay? Yup, that's the last tie,
third knot. Next week. No problem. You're welcome.

SAILOR ABOARD

Dropped the ladder over the side, climbed down,
got started scraping after chow. You get
tired stiff bacon, eggs hard, cold toast. Spotted brown,
apple I ate.
         First thing always runs out
is the lettuce, two weeks ago. Gray flakes,
rust, sifting down, there into gray water,
not clear. Sea snake starboard yesterday makes
me think if I fall.
         Worried by her letter,
hurting real bad. Me, too. Separation's tough.

Gonna be faithful when we get to port,
think of her, have a few beers. Not too thin
or thick, paint rolling off—a good brush, part
I like, nice-n-easy.
         Said she's trying, win
the lottery.
         Haul 'er up. Sea's looking rough.

SAILOR ASHORE

Some folks think a sailor's got only one
thing on his mind. A good lay. Know what I
mean? Kinda true. I mean, you get horny
as that old bull my daddy kept alone
in the back field. He'd get so mean. He'd bellow.
You gotta do *some* thin'...
                              Lots of guys the ship
crawl under covers with a sock, before sleep,
their girlfriend, so to speak a relief.
                              You know,
it was real bad before, almost died once,
living on the streets—now a job, money,
maybe a future, I'm grateful. Dunce
I used to be; no more.
                              Not everybody,
not everything's shit. For a long time I
didn't. Have a life. Now the US Navy
is what I got, now the Navy's got me.

TAILOR, MEASURING

It's not bespoke anymore, now it's just
alterations. Change from when I started,
so young, then it was a suit, jacket darted
at the waist, bagged pants, double-breasted vest.
Things change. Things don't. Everyone has one leg
longer, half, quarter inch, measure the right,
measure the left, cuffs, no cuffs. Now, too fat,
too thin, want fixed what they buy off the peg.

The handwork, I do in the back room, no light
in the place but a lamp. Sit in the chair,
the same old table where my father sat.
He was a go-getter until the Crash.
I was born, learned the trade. Without the cash
the neighborhood went down. But I'm still here.

CARPENTER

Zazen every morning at five, breakfast
at six, then I'm all ready for the day,
whatever comes.
           Workwise, in the past,
general carpentry and now recently
building cabinets. My whole thing is wood,
its nature, uniting with it to do
it right... letting it become.
           Easy, hard,
the way I press the plane has to follow
the grain, the grain teaches you how to plane.
It's timeless, I mean time passes into time,
you feel that.
           Take hammering, the difference
between nail curls or goes straight. You know Zen...
blindfolded archers hit the bull's eye they sense,

if I'm with-it, hammer's rhythm, nails are rhyme....

PROJECTIONIST

We sure aren't *The Last Picture Show*, we get
enough people to keep the place open.
I change reels by hand, no automation.
I sit up there in the booth and stay put
in case anything goes wrong. Sometimes it does,
mostly I watch the film. Last Saturday
with that afternoon rain *Pinocchio*
sold out, first thing I saw at the movies.

Then I was five and afraid of the whale.
One time at church, the preacher preached Jonah
and if he was doing what he ought to,
but he was saved, so then I was hopeful.
I like how light comes out of dark brighter,
with hues and shades that make the big picture.

GURU

Three years at Rishikesh, more at the ashram
here, and when our guru died I stayed, not
that I'm a successor; it's his spirit
in this place that makes the difference, same
as before.
          The walking stick in this case
he used until the day he passed, he knew
he would, he told us, ahead of time, true
to what he said: he would die in a place
where spiritual work of devotion
would bring love into conscious awareness.

Be still.

          Sometimes energies of bliss race
from dormancy, keep arising, and soon

I level out into a state of mind

of prayer; like, what will be well with no end.

MAILMAN

I'm on the front porch just about to put
a bunch of Christmas cards into the slot
in the storm door when I hear this voice hit
high C. "You son of a bitch." So I wait.
It gets real quiet so I push the mail
in fast and then the lady opens the door,
smiles at me sweet as pumpkin pie. "Oh, dear,"
she says, "I almost forgot this little

something for you," and hands me a bottle
of whiskey, she says, it's in a bag wrapped up nice.
You never know what goes on in a house.
Like nothing happened, I go on with my route.
They used to say, "Street angel, house devil."
None of my business, of course, who is what.

SANTA CLAUS

Ho, ho, ho, Merry Christmas, it's Santa,
what do you want for Christmas? Ringing my bell
just for you. Except the kids are gone away,
it's dinner time. Hey, old man, tell me all,
what would you like? The kids have gone away,
so I'm talking to you. Big car, new book?
Pair of slippers, a week in Florida?
Tell me, see what I can do, try your luck.

Hey, Father Brady, it's not confession,
I'm not giving penances, don't you know
who I am? I'm the policeman, Noonan,
your neighbor down the street, so ho, ho, ho,
Merry Christmas to you and Christmas cheer.
I'm almost done, wanna go have a beer?

HAIRDRESSER

Of the two, men are fussier, harder
to please. But not one has ever cried, not
here, anyway, after I finished a cut.
My friend, she permed this woman with this hair
that wouldn't perm. She tried stronger solution,
everything came out wrong, right out in hanks.
Hysteria is terrible, no thanks
for trying, or for your good intention.

I think it's the bad economy, why
people want to sue for stuff like that.
Our costs go up, we have to be insured.
Make it so my ears don't stick out, make it
flat in back, says a man. A woman might say,
I don't care what you do, just make me look good.

DRUMMER

You wouldn't believe how I got to be
a drummer. Yup, five years. I travelled here
to do a degree in gestalt psychology.
I had to learn the language, enough I'd dare
to hope a Japanese could figure what
I was saying. When another student
took me to a taiko rehearsal, it
blew me away, the drums, the minds intent
in absolute synchronized energy.
    Just a student club, but the thrill, the six
staccato drums, one big as a Suzuki,
drummers striking in sync drew me, the strokes
a blur, on-target, booming, sounded tones,
rhythms, I heard through skin, vibrating bones.

OBOIST, THINKING

The times when it sounds like a human voice,
the plaintive runs melodic, the lyric
flies from word to song and soars,
                              then a dark
will fade, a shadow glow,
                    has to, no choice
but for the human. Think times you're feeling
your body breathing, all nerves, all heart and brain
and gut.

            That breath through mouth and reed can gain
a separate life apart from me is something
could leave me reeling—wind, wood, metal, glue
(never mind ones who say its voice would tease
a duck's if a duck could learn to sing), these
elements, with others, have made a true
life possible,
            and I can think of none,
no work, more fulfilling, nor can imagine.

SAWYER

'Scuse me if I sneeze, I've been doing it
all morning, from a allergy, I guess.
That pine dust buzzes off the saw like a mess
of mini-bees on swarm. That saw will bite.

New man that don't get the hang of it can
lose a finger or worse, an old timer fights
with the wife, drinks too much too many nights.
Month ago, it was a thumb. Dropped off that man

to the floor right there. We stopped for ice cube
at the truck stop on the way to the clinic.
An hour down to the city, and they stuck
the thumb back on, sewed fine like spider web.

'Scuse me, I got to, got to... Better now.
I got to, got to go, line up that saw.

SINGER

When the lights go down and candles flicker
the tables get quiet. Piano plays
the opening bars and I'm in a blaze
of spotlight, I'm singing "Smoke Gets in Your

Eyes" pretty soon and "Fascinating Lady."
So shadowy faces pause in the dark,
for a while connect with style and music.
The crowd that comes here really listen, they

collaborate, a flow of energy,
I feel it coming back, a kind of love
their taking part, that strong. I hear someone heave
a chuckle on the upbeat or a sigh

when I tickle out a little nuance,
I feel a lost song's been found. It's my romance.

LOUNGE OWNER, 7:30 A.M.

The bar, the stools we'll put neat in a row,
and glasses lined up the overhead racks,
we'll polish the mirror behind Pernod
and Galliano and bourbon bottles. Stacks
of napkins, a bunch of stirrers... unwashed cloth
the night bartender forgot. Hours-old smells
of stale beer and leftover whiskey breath
slowly stir, and slip over the windowsills

past inches of gap into the morning.
The early birds have already wakened.
Sparrows chirp, hopping on mulch toward a tree.
A newsboy plops a paper under an awning.
A mother and child are walking hand in hand.
That nun talking on a bus looks happy.

LAUNDRY LADY

I don't have time to watch the bubbles rise
up the windows. These old machines sloshing I
know everything's all right. It's no surprise
I rely on hearing. Anything wrong, we

phone the boss. Once was a time when I could
watch the bubbles I made shine out and fly
from a dipstick, ring-end of a stick I'd
dip in soapy water. They'd float that high,

one by one bust into sudsy pieces.
Summertime we played like that, be wasting
an hour. Don't think of that nowadays. You please
excuse me while I pull that load waiting
in the dryer, dump it on the table?
She paid for folding, do it while I'm able.

ELECTRICIAN

Is it shocking? Very funny question
to ask an electrician. Rarely got
zapped worth thinking about, a few more in
my life than in my work and I forget
a time or two I blew my fuse. Divorce was
nothing I planned for, for example, nor
were triplets with my second wife; a pause
for re-organization followed both, bar
the fact that the kids were welcome, the split
wasn't—well, at the time. Later I came
to see the point. No, nothing shocking hit
me harder than those. Sure, there was the time
that new apprentice turned on the juice, bare
wire jumped, I got sizzled. My hand, here's the scar.

TRANSLATOR

Si, signore, so, I will try versions
of the verses: Leopardi, he touches
me very much; our feelings agree, yes.
Translation is treason, we Italians
say. *Allora.*
                    Just so, to know Shakespeare,
we must learn English, *si,* to feel his mind,
his heart. Just so, you feel Dante, his kind
of life, his cosmos, sphere inside sphere,
in his language, best.
                    Ma, esempio,
truly I appreciate how some who
work his triple verse try and try and try
and jump from tongue to tongue, to make beauty.
But...
           é vero? Truth, did Dante ever get
into English, words I cannot forget?

PHILOSOPHER

Where does it come from, this impulse to write?
Nothing exists without an origin,
by which it is, as it is—a sonnet
is no different. A sonnet rises from,

and by, the act of a sonneteer, yes.
But by what, from what, is a sonneteer
what he is? Consider this: artwork is
the origin of the artist (so Heidegger

teaches), the artist is the origin
of the work. Neither is, without the other.
Yet is each the only thing to sustain
the other? No. Before them both is art,
something to do with memory, mind and heart.

(Is thought like this useful, or a bother?)

PLUMBER

My degree in philosophy and now
I plumb? Sure, between then and now I learned
a little about practicalities, how
not only brain but, together, brain and hand
could make me a living and it's one I
appreciate, being self-employed where
there's always jobs—new plastic pipes work better,
easier than copper, iron rusts; see
an old house, lead pipes, I come full circle,
plumbum's the Latin word for *lead*. It's true
that Romans used it for water pipes, that they
sweetened wine with lead, their brains shrank, the fall
of empire followed. A good thing for me
I'm plumbing in an enlightened century.

HOUSE PAINTER

The old lady said since her husband died
the place's gotten shabby, sort of mess
she couldn't fix up by herself. It's less
bother to let it go until you need
to hire someone handy like me. I scrape,
first front and sides then door, doorframe, window.
Bits and scraps of sun-cracked paint flake and blow.
Summers I climb up ladders, stop and wipe

off sweat, dip brush, slap on prime, smooth out prime,
my vacation job. If English teachers
made enough, would I? Life's short. A hearse
at the house next door yesterday, gurney
rolled out with a sheet over a dead guy.
I slowed down, went home early, that one time.

PALLBEARER

A principal fifteen years, the classroom
the twenty before—since I retired, I
work part-time for a funeral company,
dark charcoal suit, dignified; I don't embalm

or anything complicated as that;
pallbearer, casket-escort, secure it
onto the gurney to the center aisle, what-
ever small service is required; a bit

of calm beside the long black hearse, nothing
intrusive. Oh, families are as different
as grief is; most hold it in at the viewing,
with friends and relatives there. Important I
remember to respect the Lord *meant*
"Let the dead bury the dead." Truthfully.

CHOIRMASTER

My degree in Voice does give me pleasure.
I keep vestry politics out of mind
and play the organ even without the choir.
Our Sunday worship brings joy to my weekend.

My favorite hymn depends on the season
and the sentiment, the voices blending.
I'm High Church, once I tried Gregorian,
Credo in Unum Day-ay-ay-um, sung

as though endless, no noticeable pause
for breath, but all possible by breathing.
Holy Breath, by the Holy Spirit, grace
amazing, I thought, hearing that choir sing.
That country church, that congregation was
unique, what happened back then, in that place.

BOXER

Started at ten, my big brother laced my mitts,
showed me, foot work, breathing right... where was I?
Yeah, didn't tap that hard, but couple hits
hurt, I got mad, opened a cut over his eye.

So, yeah, it was an accident... I stopped.
He got three stitches. Started up again
high school, more muscle on me; I popped
a kid who was State Champ and pretty soon,

I was. Not all by myself. That old coach
knew his stuff. Banged up ears, the nose, showed what
he took––yuh, fake it, watch your approach,
skip, keep your paws up, hit hard, skip back out.

So, keep in shape, will I coach? Sure. Maybe.
Who wants to fight the universe? Not me.

PLAYWRIGHT

This little theater makes it possible.
Avant garde? Crap. Amuse yourself if you
have to label. All I will say is, Tell
me that real lives have the kind of drama
structured in traditional playwrights' plays.
Look hard. No plot, random stuff is what I show,
like our everyone's-an-atom these days,
screwed up. Absurd? I'm not absurdist, no.

A realist, I think. New York's central
to our culture. Life in a tiny flat;
married to my art, so not typical,
skewed, from some people's point of view. Fat cat?

Gimme a break. I work hard, live lean.
Okay, break's over, run-through's on, again.

THINKER

There's no law you have to be consistent
toward the world, but toward yourself there is. Yes,
sir, mind inside mind watches what mind sees—
your interior observer. What event
timed a sharp instant awareness of what
times warned?
              was it in a dream this law came
or in a book? Doesn't life itself name
such acquisitions?—together head and gut

telling likely things?
              What about the flood
of dread that fills a body when a man
feels deception, untruth, falsity run,
or trickle, something not one's own, a mood
from someone not peaceful? Argue? No, simply
notice—remember yourself—leave quietly.

DENTAL HYGIENIST

I say "Open" so many times a day;
well, it gives variety. Some people,
their jaws so small and their mouths so little,
others open up so wide they could be
about to bite a whole piece of pizza
with one chomp. Of course they can't talk when I'm
scraping away the plaque. So I chatter
and go on about Little Miss Sugar Plum.

That's my Abyssinian. Her face's flat,
sort of, slightly prognathous, undershot.
Cross-breeding is why a few of her teeth
show, but, you know, as pretty as she is,
she's a mischief; pulled down our Christmas wreath,
played out her feelings with her little paws.

LANDLORD

I fix all the plumbing problems myself,
electrical, broken hinges, leaks, you
name it. Got to. Small, big: a broken shelf;
a kitchen fire; termites; rot. Got thirty,

they're small houses. Took a while to build up,
used the first one to buy the second, third,
and so on. Got to be enough to sup
with the devil, so to speak, be a landlord

full time, the thirty houses. I'm no saint,
I'm the guy it starts and ends with, I check
out contracts, new renters—when they go, paint
and patch and throw out junk. I had to deck
a drunk that came at me. I was sixty one.
After that, I collect rents, I pack a gun.

TENANT

Lived in this apartment fifteen years now.
My job at the college was for two years,
a small town, little to do, think it's why
that adjunct rode his bicycle starkers
round and round in the courtyard, Security
saw him, I got his job and now I'm still here.
The old lady downstairs, she knows I'm gay,
strict Baptist as she is, and doesn't care.

More than a good neighbor, she's a real friend.
The time my bathtub overflowed was when
we got to talking. I had to attend
to it, get the plumber. Once had a yen
to travel, but I've settled. The landlord
raised my rent only once. Isn't that good?

LIBRARIAN

A city-center library has to be...
"all things to all men"—Wasn't that St. Paul?
We serve scholars and students and people
who are homeless, mainly, here. The lobby

with the glass exhibit cases is where
homeless literates read the newspapers,
but pretty soon some're sleeping in the chairs.
Oh, I'm glad to say we don't interfere.

Our Social Justice Collection brings in
scholars from the world over, democrat,
socialist, what have you, except we won't
see the "me, me" types, they're down on Wall Street
or who knows where? But really, who knows when
or how or which're ones that care, which don't?

BANKER, TALKING

A deliberate fraud the Trickle Down is,
you said. Where'd *you* get your Economics
degree, huh? I heard you, "A bag of tricks,
of impossible lies, justifies ways
of keeping a few people rich, a lot
of people poor." Who are you to say facts
support *your* view, that politics and acts
of policy changed the balance? The market
by itself is the mechanism, I
learned at Business School.
                                        Oh, a few laws had
to change, a few decisions at the Fed,
these did not come from false beliefs as you
claim, they weren't based on metaphor someone
confused by prostate trouble had on his brain.

MODEL

The thing is, it's hard to keep looking how
they want, thin as a stick, with flexible joints,
so you swivel and jounce that model-bounce
on the catwalk, you're in sandals, stilettoes,
or barefoot, almost naked or swathed in
yards of shimmer, and your make-up won't hide
too many too-late nights. It's work. An ounce
or two more than standard emaciation
and your cheeks look puffed up like a chipmunk's.
You try out lots of veggies: cucumbers
thin-sliced in sandwiches, raw carrots, hunks
of celery, broccoli. Goodbye chicken livers,
juicy beef, chocolate, forever? Hell no!

While it lasts, though, it's not the worst way through.

GREENHOUSE GUY

Those rows of sets just starting to sprout from
the vermiculite, you know what I mean,
soil with earthworms, will raise a jungle of vine,
big red tomatoes. There's no stopping them
once they get going in this atmosphere,
like a steam room in here when we turn on
the sprinklers, well, you can feel the sun—
warm in here, not cool like that outside air.

A wonder, that power of a seed in soil,
everything natural. The care we take—
what goes in ground grows from ground,
                comes up, helps make
plants healthy. Have to put a bit of foil
around, watch for aphids, pay attention.
Is there a better way to get it done?

SECURITY GUARD

Grateful my daddy set tin cans in the yard,
at the back, that's where I got comfortable
shooting, good at it, too, could sight and feel
a bead dead right, right on, it wasn't hard.

This old mill been abandoned twenty years.
Owners got to pay tax, pay insurance.
There's acres of floor, seems like, a good chance
sometime someone'll get in, thieve, set fires.

So I got my job, night watchman kind of.
Usual quiet. Shot a rat last week,
pile of junk aside the old office in-take
fell, made me jump. The basement's the worst—
breathing through that old damp, cobweb, smell, dust.
Job's a job. Pays the bills, push comes to shove.

THEOLOGIAN

If doubt is part of faith, then I am one
faithful in my season. Watchful eye knows
the daylong span, the lifetime, of mayflies;
it sees how system can reveal reason

when mouths of fish open upsides of lakes
and close, as much as there is reason in
the way a pine in spring throws out pollen.
I watch the pear trees bloom—every twig breaks

into bud, saps from every waking root
race up the trunks, branching thin, thinner, some
thinnest. The power of a seed to become,
what is that but something no less a bet

than Pascal's? I think: does the notion "expan-
ding universe" also go to "human brain"?

MOHAWK, HIGH STEEL

Noontime, that's *my* time. I go with my lunch
off by myself. I sit down. I lean back
on a girder and open the box, crunch
away, sandwiches, cookies, milk. Noon break
is peaceful quiet. Not even a pigeon
up there, nothing between me and big sky
but high steel, crane, cable. I don't look down.
Mind my business. Never liked the city.

But there's hawks, falcons the government put
on that old skyscraper. You see them drop
like a rock, fly back, day's lunch in their claws.
I'm a country boy, we all have to eat.
Pay's good, it grows on you. Don't plan to stop
until I've got my farm, a bunch of cows.

FARMER

Well of course we do raise cows, steer, bulls, here
Our family uses a tried new method.
One day, one acre, herd two hundred head.
Grass chomped up, fields change, another acre

fertilized, goes green. So then, after cows change
fields, chickens move in, in RV-sized coops,
mobile ones with chicken-wire floors and steps
like gangplanks that drop down so they can range.

A time goes by, the chickens' droppings make
grass so rich the cows can come. The cows take a day.
They drop pies. Time. Hordes of bugs multiply.
The chickens eat. We harvest eggs. Few break.

Organic natural super-fresh, what begs
the "why of it" answers, "Good beef. Good eggs."

CASHIER

Thursdays are Senior Discount Day, only
five percent, but it helps the company
with the bottom line and the elderly
a little. My friend Marge, she wants to worry,
I guess. She gives me little bottles of
hand sanitizer. "All those germs on coins
and paper money," she goes. "OK. Enough,"
I go. "My immune system works, my genes
are good, ninety-year-olds run marathons
in my family." But what would be real good
would be those new kind of shoes, that have springs
in the heels. You bounce and teeter a little
at first, there's a learning curve, what Wilfred
my friend said, checking dollar bills at his till.

HIT MAN

The psychologist? She says I have "flat
affect." So I ask her, "What's going on?
you talking about?" She says, "You did hit
twenty people, strangled, stabbed, used a gun,

you talk about it on TV even,
not a trace of remorse or regret."
Then she stops. She goes, "No pleasure, no pain,
detectable relief how the Feds got

you immunity to incriminate
the bosses." So I don't say much; never
did, talk makes trouble. So I go, "That's right."
Every TV interviewer's after
the same stuff. They go, "You still with the mob?"
I go, "Nah. Done. Finished. It was just a job."

CONFESSOR

It's not difficult to keep the seal, at least
for me; I forget what I hear almost
at once, it's very rare it's for the first
time; most sins are not against the Holy Ghost.

They're pretty run of the mill—by which I
don't want to slight the anxiety sin,
when it's recognized, can give rise to,
or the relief confessing to someone

who'll never tell anyone can provide.
Heavy-lifting sins like murder, God knows.
Forgiveness is God's—is a way to peace.
People good and bad both have need of grace.
Human hearts' tragi-comic scenarios——
yet heaven's narrow gate can open wide.

SURROGATE

A sex surrogate does a different thing
from prostitution; it's a much newer
profession. Well, weak joke underlines pure
fact: that some people miss out on knowing

how—how to be comfortable with bodies,
their own and when they're with another person—
a kind of trance that needs to be woken
from—our whole tone and attitude, purpose

and consequence is remedial. Yes,
I am certified as a surrogate.
And yes, I'm married. My husband's so great,
the best person I'll ever know. He knows
I'm professional helping many men,
these years. It's my work. He respects it. Amen.

LAWYER

I couldn't even pretend to laugh at
that foolish little clichéd pseudo-pun.
Lawyer/liar surely means only one
thing, that a lawyer will take any part.

I'm pro-bono, part-time, in such a case
it means I don't charge, I don't need the pay.
No, no private means. During law school I
worked, teaching. Do still. Couldn't turn my face

from kids who need to learn what words will do,
how right, well-ordered words can determine
an outcome in court or classroom—can shine
a light on life itself when words are true.

Our life goes deeper than words, like nuance
that lives between brief lines in a silence.

STILT WALKER

I bring my own stilts and striped green trousers,
and get barely more than minimum wage.
I'm up too high to get tips. People gauge
the height, and stay clear in case I fall. Worse is,
a big advertisement on my back wears
me out—not worth the few bucks extra, weird
to feel so fatigued after. Bro, it tears
at my self-esteem being a walking bill-board.

My attitude's persistent. You'd see me,
the kid who makes practice perfect, walking
my stilts around the yard, grownup's hobby
before it came to be, there, in the making.

A change, these Saturdays; my cubicle
weeks fade away I'm all in air and tall.

PERSONAL TRAINER

I've been working out like this ever since
I found the Charles Atlas worksheets my brother
left behind when he got hitched. That winter
I stayed indoors working my muscles, Tense
and Release, that plain Dynamic Tension
is how I got my natural shape, not
too massive, not too ripped.
                                        I like to set
a client on the right program, he can
stay healthy into old age. Ninety-two,
this guy who couldn't do a single push-up
when he was *eighty*-two, is a champ now.
He looks great, feels great—he won a Master's cup,
the Seniors. Retired insurance broker.
He beat the actuaries fair and square.

CLOWN

Happy and sad are only two of my
faces, I have more under the make-up.

Fresh out of college, I was twenty-three—
didn't know what to do for the next step.

What did you want to do when you were ten?
I asked myself. Maybe that was how I
knew what would work. I mean, for me. So when
I went to Clown School here in Florida

to be a clown, I learned routines, could keep
in sync with prancing horses, acrobats,
the elephants, little white poodles that leap,
the brass band's energy, the ringmaster's spats.

But what I remember most is the kids scared
of clowns. Smiles, tears, part-time now, still paired.

JUGGLER

Juggling's easy? A juggler can't hide his slips.

I know, hey, everyone juggles—budgets,
schedules, complicated relationships.
But how about placing eleven plates,

whirling them along your arms, chin, forehead,
your feet, while lighted candles flip from hand
to hand and keep their flame? Am I afraid
I'll lose concentration, my peaceful mind?

Man, I dropped enough, broke enough, before.
Almost lost my nerve the time they shattered,
blue white red plate after plate, on the floor.
That audience—half laughed, half booed—mattered
to me, for a while I lost faith, okay?

Try it? Here. Three oranges. Give it a go.

FISHERMAN

No deep sea, nothing like that, no ocean.
My uncle, y'know what happened. Caught his thumb
winching, hauling net. Lost his life goddam
later. I like ashore. I cast a line
from here, here on the beach, I see a flash,
a fish running, my reel whizzing—my bait!
The blues-run end of summer you can wait
all night out here, quiet time, hear 'em splash.

Easy to take the fish for granted. I don't.
I'm grateful. Every one counts. Our dinner,
what I carry home, protein on the dish.
Part time job in a way. Saves money I wish
I had, but don't. It's seasonal, thinner
catch nowadays used to be abundant.

FRESHMAN

Getting used to time management, I guess.
Has been, like, not that high school I just let things
happen, okay? Studious, tried my wings—
languages, art, dance, painting, a mess
of good stuff. Yo, long story short, I was a geek
then and am still. Like, now I'm into software, how
code in the program can tweak something to go
even when it started odd, not that a freak
for art like me is immune. Anyway,
you know what? It could be love, like—not sure,
but I met someone in freshman English.
Other side, there're student loans. I wish
I didn't have to borrow, have to care
the job market gets better in time for me.

IT Work-Study Assistant

The Help Desk is where staff and students come.
Otherwise we go to office, classroom,
the support center, bookstore. Choice of farm
or programming. Its old dust needs a new broom,
my granny told me that. I ain't one to fret
a man's got to do what his dad did, follow
along like the world's the same as when it
isn't, as if up there in our hollow
behind the hill an old cabin couldn't
grow a kid like me into a techie.
Always liked numbers, fixing things, a bent
for solving. Professor's voicemail just now,
couldn't download a poem about a green fuse;
always something to learn; to me that's good news.

SOPHOMORE

So, yes, opportunities here do give
me feelings of hope and inspiration.
Sophomore slump? not like a real big question.
Here, in second year, we're seniors. I live

at home, work part-time, keep expenses low.
A community college does so much
for people, like in my painting class, such
a diversity. I'm twenty, at my elbow,

next easel, a student might be sixty
or eighty or thirty. The professor herself's
ageless, seventy-five or whatever,
young/old at the same time, savvy, real nice.

Gotta go. A gig in the city tonight,
singing a new song, some guitar and lute.

PROSPECTOR

Using a lump of rock for a door stop,
they were, a long time, it was mostly gold.
Found out when the grandkid gave a right tap,
a hammer, some old crud fell off and told

the tale. Already digging thereabouts
I wasn't more welcome after. Up here
folks like to keep themselves to themselves, roots
matter, careful sensible folks don't share

what's not in their interest to. Understand,
that's not criticism, it's right stupid
to trust just any stranger coming up

the way. My permit lets me dig on land
that's public. No nine to five, I abide—
the backcountry, crackin' rocks in a gap.

EQUESTRIENNE

Blonde bun smooth beneath her black safety helmet,
in her black tailored coat, firmly seated,
she guides her gleaming chestnut Thoroughbred,
each poised, responding to a common thought.
He accelerates, imperceptibly slows
before each jump, takes to air, forelegs tight,
and lightly they sail over—he follows
the course, clearing rails and ditches—upright
rider, outstretched horse, while the crowd watches.

Now, every day they post in close rhythm,
horse and rider—there are days she catches
her breath, they gallop, hair and mane like flame
racing a wind.
        Mornings, she's up at five,
she mucks out his stall. She's glad. She's alive.

ACTOR

You know what is valued changes the sense.

To be an actor is respected today.
But in the past there was a big difference.

In the Middle Ages an actor like me,
when he died, was not allowed burial.

It was asked if anyone who could be
so many others had a single soul—
an identity question, in logic so

cerebral, abstract. I ask, Couldn't they
see it the other way? That we are souls
embodied? What are we but energy
materialized? Oh, never mind. Fools
will tread. Angels will fly. Like Peter Pan
I drop in. But will grow old, do what I can.

ARCHAEOLOGIST

We were kids watching them dig the big hole.
They left at the end of the day, then my friend
and I climbed down. I picked up a shovel.
A red and brown shard stuck out from the ground.

I still have some broken bits of the pot.
The clay could have been fired a week before,
it looked that new. Now I know I was right
to save the shards under the attic floor.

When I returned from Egypt that first time,
there they were in the attic, I found them.
Picking them up was like a waking dream.
I saw the boy I was, man I became.

Images become facts after a while.
I found a life in tombs beside the Nile.

BILLIONAIRE

My only luxury, as I see it,
is the Jacuzzi in the jumbo jet,
the plane itself is a necessity (yet
my wife complains, she says it's a "his," nit-

picking at me, and wants a "hers"). First
time I had a billion, I felt fulfilled
for a while, then made more, then more. Then, would
you believe, I lost balance between best

and good—losing time I can't replace to
build wealth I can get more of, up markets
or down.
        Recent blood tests showed weird platelets.

And when I feel tired, I know what to do—
keep making money, it's how I feel good.

My business will carry on when I'm dead.

BANKER, BANKING

Why shouldn't a banker be Secretary
of the Treasury? Conflict of interest
be damned—makes sense that guys who make money
understand what to do, that they're the best

choice to do interface between Wall Street
and the ninety-nine percent. You complain.
Look, people on minimum wage, they get
fifteen grand a year, some CEOs gain

five hundred thousand a day, so what's new?
The return of robber barons, you say,
a Golden Age that's golden for a few.
Give yourself a break, don't fight it, the lay
of the land is survival—we know who's
fittest the more we see whose money grows.

WAITRESS

Twenty years, never been like this, people
are really hurting, every booth full of
customers a year ago. Now it's real,
real slow. You both decided, what you'll have?

Healthy? The fruit salad is big, very,
it's slimming, customers like it. Try it?
You can see, no one at the bar, every
booth, table, empty but this one and that.

Is everything okay? Little water?
Been too hot this week, I hope it cools off.
Our tomatoes are drooping, my daughter.
Just phoned her, eleven, keep up with stuff.

More coffee? The milk sherbet hit the spot?
Thank you. The check? Come back. Have a good night.

TEMP, ENDING

Wait a minute, I've got a call, think what
I should do, my last day.... The resumé
got me a spot on a Greenpeace ship, free-
lance sort of. I mean, too soon to say it
will lead anywhere closer than sailing
the Antarctic sea.... Sir, the gentleman
you want has left the firm. Personnel? When
he left?
      I'm back. Something about whaling,
documenting, be doing video,
some writing. No. No, haven't thought about
danger much. Just a sec, got a call, shout,
yell, have a ball.... Same one, wanting to know,
from me, something I don't. Anyhow, great.
Good. Thanks. Great. Friday night let's celebrate.

People from every social class (every socio-economic class) work. *Working Voices* do not rise from one sector of the society only. The expression "working class" is a hold-over from earlier centuries when there existed a co-valent leisure class, a socio-economic system a version of which the currently popular TV program *Downton Abbey* dramatizes. Nowadays, people at all income and educational levels work, from hard-working billionaires to the unemployed who have the difficult work of seeking and finding jobs in an outsourcing economy. Today, we all work, all our voices are working voices. At the same time, extreme inequalities that remain uncorrected, engender a hollowing out of the socio-economic body. We are all "here" in actual connection. Connectivity counsels us that "working together" is plain English for "co-operation." Is it not possible, is it not reasonable, that the Constitution's declared grounding fact, "We, the People," its opening words, be understood as another name for Solidarity, people who raise voices and work in mutual responsibility for ourselves and one another?

ABOUT THE AUTHOR

Thomas Heffernan received an *Atlantic* National Collegiate Award for Essay, a National Endowment for the Arts Literary Fellowship in Poetry and Fiction awarded through the Southern Arts Association, the Roanoke-Chowan Award (for *The Liam Poems),* the Kusamakura Grand Prize as well as Mainichi distinctions for haiku, and the Sam Ragan Award. Following assignments in the North Carolina Poetry-in-the-Schools program, he served as a Visiting Artist in the NC Arts Council/NC Dept. of Community Colleges program. Co-founder of the Martha's Vineyard Writers Workshop held during several summers in August, in Japan he later co-edited *Plover/Chidori*, a bi-lingual haiku magazine. He earned his A.B. at Boston College, his M.A. at Manchester University in England, his Ph.D. at Sophia University, Tokyo, all in English Literature. He has taught at universities in the United States, England and Japan, and aboard ship in the U.S. Navy PACE program for afloat college education. Currently he lectures at the University of North Carolina, Pembroke.

Index of Titles

Proof

Made in the USA
Charleston, SC
08 September 2015